WEEMOED

TIM DOOLEY

WEEMOED

PBS WINTER RECOMMENDATION

 **EYEWEAR** PUBLISHING

First published in 2017
by Eyewear Publishing Ltd
Suite 333, 19-21 Crawford Street
Marylebone, London w1h 1pj
United Kingdom

Cover photograph and design, and typeset by Edwin Smet
Author photograph by David Hunter
Printed in England by TJ International Ltd, Padstow, Cornwall

ISBN 978-1-911335-97-9

*Eyewear wishes to thank Jonathan Wonham for his
generous patronage of our press.*

WWW.EYEWEARPUBLISHING.COM

For Ben and Sam
and for Connie, Liam and Josef

TIM DOOLEY

is a tutor for The Poetry School
and a visiting lecturer at the University of Westminster.
He was a teacher for many years and has been an Arts Mentor
for the Koestler Trust. From 2008 to 2017 he was reviews and
features editor of *Poetry London*. He is co-editor (with Martha
Kapos) of *The Best of Poetry London* (Carcanet, 2014). His first
collection of poems, *The Interrupted Dream,* was published by
Anvil in 1985. This was followed by the pamphlets *The Secret
Ministry* (2001) and *Tenderness* (2004), both winners in the
Smith/Doorstop–Poetry Business pamphlet competition.
Tenderness was also a Poetry Book Society Pamphlet Choice.
Keeping Time (Salt, 2008) was a Poetry Book Society
Recommendation and was followed by *Imagined Rooms*
(Salt, 2010). *The Sound We Make Ourselves:
Poems 1971-2016* was published
by Eyewear in 2016.

TABLE OF CONTENTS

FAN-PIECE

after Huangfu Ran

Because in every crowd
I would search for my parents'
faces, I've come where
clouds cover the ragged peaks
of the far mountains
to burn incense and recall
wisdom I once heard.

The mountains form a dense wall.
From the old temple
I watch petals of snow pile
one on another
bringing blankness everywhere.

A FLOATING LIFE

Joys of the Wedding Chamber

That year of different furnished rooms
in villages and small towns to the South,
making ourselves known to one another
in a shared single bed, its dismantled
partner leaning upright on the wall.

Pleasures of Leisure

Saturday. The slow train to the river.
Across the meadow to the bankside path.
Safely moored, the boats bob up and down.
Trying out the manners of the privileged,
the summer evening never seems to end.

Sorrows of Misfortune

Look for a place. Seek disappointment.
Mean well. Discover spite and suspicion.
A crumpled face. Chill in the stomach.
The nervous tremor. It all takes you back
to loss and the memory of loss.

Delights of Roaming Afar

Gulls over the valley catch the light
like feathers shaken from a pillow.
Pine trees like exclamation points.
We breathe in their rich scent listening
for the low bass shrieking of the frogs.

MEETING i

I would have been just eighteen
that summer before college   A levels
finished weeks ago   a kind of giggling
freedom   spreading from friend to friend
that July Saturday   we marched around
the tennis court   chanting anti-
apartheid slogans   It wasn't quite the
levitation of the Pentagon   but it caused
a sort of stir   the Davis cup disrupted
and the start of 'Stop the 70 Tour'

When we turned the corner   you were
there late again   with crooked grin
and cigarette
     and when a cheer broke out
     we nearly got you arrested
they took you to sit in a coach
thinking you   flour-bombed the court
halting the match   the respectable
spectators   spat on us from the stands
     on a day of hope and laughter

So when your face comes now   in
a dream or memory   it is that startled
look that surfaces   puzzled absurdity
that will not be repressed   sensing the
ridiculous fate that waits for us   like
the childhood stroke   that scarred your
brain   and took you away   barely in
middle age   we live where anything can
happen   says the hand waving smoke
     say the blue and dancing eyes

LOWESTOFT

The engine cooled. Light
stole from the sky, as though
the week behind disgusted it.

He could have turned away
then, taken his cracked
life to some unlovely spot

where sea winds seem to
disinfect failed promise, and
made himself unknown.

Instead he walks the bright
aisles of the store, poking in
freezer cabinets and scanning

shelves, collecting onions,
bacon, potatoes, shellfish, cod
and herbs, his own salt air.

AT THE COAST

i

What we can see and name is subject to change.
Land and water have become as malleable as sky.
If we read from left to right, or from the bottom corner to the top,
with neck stretched back, the text is unstable.
The cobalt streak announces itself as a headland now.
In an hour it will be muddied in rising mist.
Even a few steps forward reveal a different pattern along the shoreline.

ii

We have reached the end of land.
Here old explorers might have gazed at the curve of sea and sky
and seen, beyond gradations of light and colour, such glimmers
          of promise.

We look back along the bay's curve at headlands fading one by one.
Detail gradually gives way to form alone, vague in its shading,
like memory with its gaps.

iii

This monochrome photo must be from the 1950s.
The sky, seen left to right, reads indifferently as pale.
At its bottom edge, I make out the wispy outline of a fence.
Below that the powdery grey and stony black
of a rock face falling from a field.
To the left, the corner of a striped awning explains
the intent gaze of the young crowd facing it.

iv

At first I only notice the boys.
There are girls' faces in the middle rows, but the boys dominate the scene.
At the back, a father lifts a toddler, in pixie hood and reins,
to catch sight of the show.
Another man, in cricket jumper, tie and blazer, leans his head.
The boys wear short trousers, coats and jumpers; some wear ties;
two boys wear caps, one flat. Is it a Sunday?
And in the front row: here we are.

v

From left to right a cousin and two brothers descend diagonally by height.
Our eyes point right and up against the gradient of our stance.
You can read abstractions in the faces:
pity, fascination, fear.

But what shock makes them so intent?
The pantomime violence of baby, policeman, devil?
Or the appalling waste of sausages?

vi

Between here and the retreating sea, in the ordinary
beauty of a bank holiday Monday, the only
slightly oil-stained sand supports pink-shovelled
excavating toys, dogs shaking spray,
and volley-balling girls wearing bands of Day-Glo citrus.

Cradling on a ledge like nesting birds, teenagers sip from cans
above caves I crawled through as a child.

A few feet from the waves, my father puts spin
on a tennis ball, playing cricket with my sons.

I'm watching from a deckchair inside a memory,
knowing how soon this day will end.

vii

We sit on the wall where the beach meets the road.
Today all is colour:
the stripes of the professor's tent,
the Punch and Judy finger puppets hanging ready for sale,
toddlers in summer outfits, laughing or stretched out on the sand.

It is the deck chair attendant wanting his fee
that scatters the peace, the mother refusing to pay
and scooping her charges away.

viii

In the steel twilight between where we stand and the opposing bank,
a small island emerges, or a large group of rocks
hardly bigger in sight than this rock plant's lilac petals.
Here a light stands sending its beams up and down the estuary.
Ships pass on necessary journeys
watching out for kirk and harbour and home.

ix

Looking north and east from the stony beach
to Sheppey and the turbines of the Kentish Flats,
we watch evening perform its usual alchemy, shifting each minute.

The reddening point of light, just now a silver disc,
leaks to a horizontal smear at the edge of the island.

A pool of white on the stillish northern sea
reflects a pale blue gap between the sky's pale and darker greys.

Two girls scoop pebbles into plastic buckets.

x

A stream runs down to the cove between clefts of rock.
Long centuries announce themselves in rock folds left to right.
The boy splashes in the little stream that runs by the beach café.
A red-faced father shouts to him to stop.
We try not to show we are looking,
just as the boy pretends not to have heard.

Rage grows in the man as the boy steps, indifferent, away.
He hands ices to the boy's sisters and turns from them sharply.
The boy leans on the fence and holds his stare.
The father puts the third ice in the recycling bin.
The boy turns to the sea, hearing the music
of everything that has happened before.

xi

In Margate this summer, in the Tracy Emin show,
'She Lay Down Beneath the Sea', facing the English Channel
in the corner of an upstairs room, is a work called 'Dead Sea'.

A rust-striped Heals mattress sports a large surf-coloured stain.
A bronze branch forked like a dowser's rod rests on the makeshift bed.
Light from the sea plays over it.

xii

The scattered sheep are feeding on the deep green fields.
At Beachy Head, two bicycles: one upright, one lying on the grass.
The pure white of the cliff is broken here and there by mosses
and scars of yellow earth as it stretches down,
giving way at the sea's edge to a lighthouse
painted in bands of red and white like a child's toy, or barber's pole.

xiii

The white page and the lamp's pool
of light can't hold me when I know
that gulls taste the drunkenness
of spray scattered in an unknown sky.

So Mallarmé (or something like)
longing to dunk his heart in the sea.
The steamer in the bay, the sailor's
songs, calling a hundred miles inland.

xiv

In Truffaut's *400 Coups* there is a moment
when the screen fills with the faces of children.
Some laugh, some gasp or scream, one places his hands over his ears.
In the reverse shot we see puppets of Redcap and the Wolf,
the woodman with his truncheon. In the cinema
we stare at the children's faces staring out at us
as Antoine and René plan their escape to the sea.

xv

And out beyond the mobile homes
the skylark's vanishing song
stretched high above us to the clouds
as we waited to hear it again.

In Sisley's picture it is called Lady's Bay.
We knew it as Rotherslade –
the little bay between the headland and the hotel
with the ruined dance hall you remembered from the twenties.

It's not there in Sisley's picture.
A few figures look at the breakers mounting the rust-coloured rocks.
In the distance are a half-dozen sails and some smudges of smoke.
In our time we saw super-tankers heading for the docks.
You remembered ships taking coal to Australia.

The dance hall café isn't in the painting
and I read it's not there now, cleared for the millennium.
We look into the middle distance,
waiting to see it again.

Sisley painted Rotherslade in 1897,
the year of the Assam earthquake
and the opening of the Blackwall Tunnel,
the year Sir John Jackson gained permission
to dredge the waters east of Start Point.

The fishermen of Hallsands built their houses
on compacted sand, or rock spurs in the cliff
that sheltered them from the prevailing wind.
Newfoundland dogs were trained to swim out to a boat
in poor weather, take a rope, and pull it up the sand.

Sixteen hundred tons of sand and gravel were removed each day.
The level of the beach fell by about twelve foot.
The absence of a single powerful landowner
may have meant that opposition to the dredging
and claims for compensation were relatively weak.

Twenty years of this, high tides and an Easterly gale
combined to destroy the village.
The families gathered in the London Inn,
the year of Passchendaele
and the October revolution.

xviii

Though it is August, there are few swimmers this morning.
It has been a summer of rain, of cloud and the threat of rain.
A few groups gather at the sea's edge.

A woman and two girls look up at the taller well-built man,
who dances for them where the water laps and stains the sand,
making them laugh as he shifts his balance lightly
from bare ankle to prosthetic lower leg.

xix

Salt on the tongue, the scent of seaweed
as we stumble on uneven ground,
the beach at night calls us
at any age as a thing forbidden.

Lights in the distance
and lights reflected on the shifting surface;
the withdrawing roar
an invitation to dance.

xx

Walking the coastal path, we cannot miss
the monumental pillars that sea has carved from chalk.
The eye also favours stubborn grasses,
Bird's-foot Trefoil and Queen Ann's Lace
clinging to unpromising earth.

As children, we scrambled up rocks
hunting the rare advantage of height.
Now we walk towards the afternoon sun
letting land and sea reveal themselves:
a mystery plotted with shade and light.

MORNING

It was the old man's idea to put the poems in the airing
cupboard; twinkling, non-committal, he slid away
from us, but there was an abiding sense that
preservation was an issue.

And now these loose sheets are yellowing and
tinged with fire.

I start to search for a bound volume where another
version could exist, while the girl already holds
a rescued page between the palms of outstretched
hands, blowing on it coolly and starting to recite.

Her voice is rich and steady and is already merging
with the World Service correspondent's measured
assessment of change.

It is possible to be too well informed.

A bird signals in morse, repeats itself, flings off a
rapid flurry of notes and waits silent in the darkly
unresponding air.

If one is patient, a half-light emerges and eventually
the hard lines of your calling.

And that is the world you enter with your ice-scraper.

LITTLE POEM

Baudelaire admired the astonishing harmony of life in capital cities,
a harmony maintained in the tumult of human identity.

And there have been days when I walked into Oxford Street ready to
sing the body electric, to absorb its volume, its clashing singularity.

But mostly I head for the side turnings and lanes where a button-shop
still survives, or the headquarters of a private and learned society.

It is not a world I belong in, but it is one where I can pass unmarked.

IT WAS A CIRCUS,

he said. (The marriage.) And
hardly were those words out
when the vision of a spangled
diamanté thigh dandled
from a chandelier imposed
itself – and in the kitchen
sword-swallowers, dodging
the aerialists' flambeaux, forgot

their macrobiotic instructions;
was he thinking of the clowns
with their surgically adjusted
smiles, on a mission to put
their own face on every face
and make small children cry?

SWAN SONG

Plusieurs Sonnets, Stéphane Mallarmé

i

Desire. And ache down the spine. I'm wasting
away in the shadows. The dream goes black.
A final warning. The bright wing retracts
inside me – the dark, infallible wing.

This wealth in wood-panelled rooms while curling
leaves on the bank's atrium trees dry back,
leaving a liar's pride in the steady black
of the preacher's eye – brain-blown with believing.

But yes, at the back end of night, a universe
could flame forth its secrets in a burst
of light unfiltered by the age's grimness

and Space, expanding, collapsed – as we know
it is – could in this weak streetlamp's dimness
witness some star-birth's centuries-old show.

ii

Can what's fresh and vital in this sweet day
free us with a wing's beat, a drunk's loose tongue,
from a hidden lake, from a frozen ring,
a stalled world, where no flight can fly away?

The mythical swan recalls its display –
off, launched without hope, and proudly wheeling
over land he failed to mark with singing
when the dull spring was broken this bright day.

That long neck emerges from the white pain
Space inflicts on those that shatter its frame,
but the bird's feathers seem horribly stained.

Brilliance, pure light, brought this unreal, fine
presence here, frozen in dream, shamed, constrained
by exile. The swan, screeching its own sign.

iii

He left us. The suicide with the light
in his face, with trails of glory, bright gold-
lettered laughter, brave battle colours rolled
out to mark (say it) my own grave's site.

There's nothing left from the tempest's blazing height.
No solemn joys. The pumping blood runs cold.
No brands are lit. The only rays your old
head provides – treasured, caressed delight.

My constant, nonchalant star, it's you keep
the light that vanished from the sky, the leap
of a young girl's pride in her glowing hair.

On the pillow its brightness imposes
as if a child-empress's crown lay there.
Your simile: a shower of roses.

iv

I raise for you this poet's box of tricks,
fearless, high like the lighthouse of Pharos,
a votive offering to the burning Phoenix,
ashes you can't store in an amphora.

Imagine an empty room, an onyx
jar on a side table. The sonorous
breath of mourning, tears, waters of the Styx.
The only object Nothingness honours.

Between the leaded casement's sloping bars
a gold light flits across the painted door
and fire-fleeing unicorns in books.

She who once stood naked in the mirror
has vanished. And in the frame is fixed
the constellation of the seven stars.

THE DIFFICULTY OF SIGHT

I cannot look long at the seafront hotels. The white walls
project sunlight as much as reflect it.

If the servants of the state form a phalanx around the flame,
do not admit that they own it.

The proofreader's pencil can't shade your decisions.
Push on to the final word.

The ants are dragging dead comrades back to the colony.
I anthropomorphize what is only accumulation of matter.

As is the giant bay tree outside the classroom, whose leaves
pattern the figures passing beneath.

Bleached by autumn, his words fall away from him like the
titles of books shelved in sunlight under glass.

We are drawn to the tallest stretch of sky, to windows that
track untroubled light as it climbs the side of a building.

RESPONSIBILITIES

Here she is outside the supermarket,
one hand cradling her face, the other pulling
tightly at the neck of her gabardine coat.

I take her to the coffee shop where, somehow,
you know what to say. I offer a telephone number,
'Was that wise?', you seem to ask.

Which makes us late for the reception.
'I haven't trained for this', you advise,
eyeing the champagne anxiously.

'Do I talk to him?', I respond.
His white suit and bow tie fool no-one.
Or are there limitations to disgrace?

It's perfectly reasonable that I should be asked
to cook chicken paprika out here in the street,
but what is the fish doing in my outstretched hands?

Luckily the boys are here to help
remove stock from the closed-down record store.
They are filling the milk float nicely.

It's a pity that someone has taken off the handbrake,
that it's rolling backward towards the river,
that I can't seem to gesture for help through these bars.

Vincent Van Gogh, *Royal Road, Ramsgate* (1876)

WEEMOED

Weemoed (melancholy) may be a good experience, provided we write it as two words: *wee* (woe), which is in every man, each of us having reason enough, but it must be allied to *moed* (courage), and the more the better for it is good to be someone who never despairs.

— *Letters,* Vincent Van Gogh

i

Before the summer started, but on a day when
rain and spray had given up their competition
and streaks of light were starting to cut through
the varied grey, I was in the Belgian Café
along Ramsgate harbour, with its unmatched,
second-hand furniture and amateur paintings,
waiting for the fish soup to arrive. They were
unloading crates from a transit. Fresh from
the hovercraft crossing, I thought. A girl
with a dog came in – pale, shaking, and asking
for water. The young pair from the bar seemed
to know her, sat her down, brought her a glass
and a bowl for the dog. They were tender with
the creature, praising its coat and calm, as if to
sustain what fortitude survived in her hardly
held together state.
            And it wasn't far from here
the Dutchman had started out teaching the boys
of Mr Stokes's academy. His drawing, of the view
from the window in Royal Road, the window
they looked through when their parents left,
shows streetlamps, a promenade, a fishing boat,
gulls struggling against the evening wind, an inn.

And in a letter he describes the rainy dusk when
lamps are lit and their light reflected in the wet.
When the boys offended Mr Stokes and were
forbidden bread and tea, their melancholy looks
at the broken pane grew longer and more longing.
He hoped to stay the winter.

ii

We were beginning our working lives and our lives together.
I'm thinking of decades ago, the start of the Seventies.
I was learning to teach at the Boys' Secondary Modern,
between Ramsgate station and the shorefront, while you
worked inland at the school in the mining village.

The Snowdown Pit was dug before the First World War
and the village where you worked was built in 1926.
Miners blacklisted at home after the General Strike
came from the Rhondda, Lanark or Durham and settled here.
It would close in the 1980s, one year after the final strike.

In the Borinage, the lay preacher who will some day be a painter
admires the working people he has found himself among –
'when Paul has a vision of a man from Macedonia begging him
to come to him in Philippi, we should think of the Macedonian
as a workman, with lines of sorrow and suffering in his face'.

The region is the subject of *Misère au Borinage*, a film from
1933 by Joris Ivens and Henri Storck. Striking men forage
for loose coal chippings left among the slag. One hooded figure,
a sack on his back, shuffles home to a roof of corrugated iron.
Now it powers data servers for Google in giant stacks.

iii

'By the sadness of the countenance
the heart is made better'. He considers
the life of *un homme intérieur et
spirituel* as a possible career.

There are forces against this.
In the radio discussion
the possession of a 'wandering mind'
has just been described as 'a condition'.

iv

One short-lit Saturday in the bleak end of the year,
you unclip the car-park trolley and splash into the store.
As you wheel towards optimal displays of the world's fruits
the left edge of your sight catches the gathering line

at the tobacco kiosk. It's not a queue for cigarettes.
Variously clad but oddly cheerful, tapping a foot
perhaps with impatience, eager and alert they stand,
taking their place among Powerball and Rollover signs.

In a sketch for a water-colour, he catches the group
outside Moojiman's State Lottery in The Hague.
From their backs – shawled women, men in caps,
a solitary top hat – the sense of expectation is evident.

A loose semi-circle narrows entering the porch,
as if the inverse of a congregation spilling out of church.
You need to think about a group, he writes,
to know what you are looking at. This man in Tesco

with the thin yellow rain-jacket and pale blue jeans,
you can't tell what he does or how he lives, but
you know an air of freedom hangs about him – an
innocence about what wealth is and what it does.

v

Like a letter in an illuminated manuscript,
a study for a lithograph in the English style:
her long brown hair unbraiding along her back,
small hanging breasts, face hidden in the fold
of her thin arms as if in penitence. Her belly
is beginning to swell. She is in mid-term and
sits on a stump, more naked than nude. On the
bare flat earth a few stubborn flowers, crocuses
or a snowdrop perhaps, and branches yet to bud.
He adds a line from Michelet and, in English,
the word 'Sorrow'. He has made an object of
this woman he has tried to love in a muddle
of charity and desire. What he wants is to make
a home: these images of the swaddled child
in its basket by the stove. When they can't
support each other or the child, the two will
part and she, Sien, outlive him twenty years.

vi

The chance to publish,
to put these exhalations
of the self in order.

A justification? No a
challenge to those who
offer an exasperated sigh.

A group portrait where
he is an unexpected
visitor at the meal.

The oil lamp shakes,
tea is poured into
small handleless cups.

They reach with forks
towards the small tubers
that fill the shared plate.

Is this a place
that would accept him?

vii

In Earls Court Square or
Lambs Conduit Street,
I watched the poets

searching among their
agile-minded, nervous
familiars for friends,

fellow-travellers at least,
as loyalties and jealousies
were shaped and shifted.

Was Paris that different,
sitting at the back of
Cormon's atelier in

an era of isms? How to
follow *La Grande Jatte*?
How to know who to trust
in the little boulevard?

viii

The equipment of art:
off-the-peg canvases,
prodigal supplies of paint
applied over and over.

He sees how things
are formed by the use
we give them – these
boots smeared with

the touch of outside,
leather warped to the
wearer's given shape,
laces frayed by tying

and untying, over
and over again – the
work prepared for
and after undone.

ix

We can catch the TGV at Lille, provenance
Brussels – destination Nice. It will zigzag
down the length of France, taking in factories,
distribution depots, villages, cream-white cows
scattered across broad green fields, grain stores,
orchards, gradually more rolling fields of
patchwork colour, geometric housing estates,
a city of insurance offices and corporate
pagodas – all of this punctuated by trench-like
embankments – until red-roofed farmhouses
flash past between craggy limestone outcrops
and cypresses staggering sideways over fields.

x

In my last year at school
in an unseen poetry exam,
along with a piece by Blake
and another by someone
whose name I forget,
was Allen Ginsberg's
poem about the railroad
hay flower's 'soiled
dry center cotton tuft
like a used shaving
brush that's been lying
under the garage for a year'.

I hadn't looked that much
at flowers then, happier
with the sunflower, say,
as a symbol or device –
and, I suppose, surprised,
when I saw a group of them,
large but raggedly
unspectacular in a small
front garden tub.

It takes some living
to begin to sense these
flashes of colour or scent
as having to do with
the world we populate
with hopes and fears.
Perhaps I could start
with these harebells,
I thought, pale and
almost transparent,
waving undefended
at the feet of trees.

xi

To gather a dozen or more blooms in an earthenware vase
is a statement of sorts. He works at the large flowers
from sunrise, doing the whole thing in one go.
He knows they will wilt quickly.

He does this every day with the idea of welcoming a friend,
making a room for a guest, a fellow artist, someone
who will share with him this daily attention
to the necessary process of dying.

He imagines a dozen or more panels like windows in a church,
aspiring to the condition of music, broken yellows
bursting from backgrounds of pale or deeper blue
framed with thin laths painted in orange.

Nothing but large flowers. Like the ones in the restaurant
next to his brother's shop. Flowers in bud or gone to seed.
Flowers in a yellow vase. He hopes this will be best.
Light against light.

Yellow of sunlight. Yellow of gaslight. Veronese blue.
There is earth also in their muddy brown corollas.
Some stalks are lollipop-firm, some drooping reveal
the vivid green of their underparts.

So Gauguin, who hated all this yellow waste of paint
took two canvases with him when,
as everyone knows,
it fell apart.

Something, he must have calculated,
could be salvaged from the mess.

xii

When we arrive in Arles,
the fair is setting up
between the station
and the Rhône. We cut
across the cables and
follow the curve of
the wide river into town.

A new museum is open,
with film of a performance
painter capturing his
Arlesienne live in the
marketplace; a fan's
collection of ephemera –
hideously miscoloured
postcards, quotations
and an absinthe bottle
with the artist's face.
Panels of coloured glass
pattern the sunlight in
the stairwell. On the walls
prints of Hiroshige, like
those he bought in Antwerp
and Paris, and canvases
by Mauve and Monticelli
precede a few of his own,
the sulky Zouave and, still
vivid in its shocking yellow,
the battered house of his
last hopes. In the courtyard
a young Chinese couple
photograph their smiling
solitary son next to the
white gates that split the
trademark signature in two.
It is a kind of victory.

THE TEMPEST (PERCY STOW, 1908)

It starts, or what survives of it starts, suddenly.
He is winched into the boat with his girl and his book.
He carries her among rocks that no-one could mistake for rocks.
And is more frightened than his child.

When he sees another child, a wild abandoned child
who grubs among grasses for food,
he holds the wild-eyed boy to his will with a stick
and is suddenly less frightened.

Now he can dream of a second girl, half Alice
half fairy-friend of Conan Doyle, who can play
the magic tricks of the Meliès picture house,
turning to fox, jumping in and out of the frame.

Now he is a Music Hall trickster with his smoke and doves.
His girl a grown beauty. The satin gown
must be green, with its pre-Raphaelite sleeves.
In the opening crack of the cave, a ship splits and drowns.

And here comes a brave form, a gorgeous gentleman.
His feathered hat, being drenched in the sea,
holds notwithstanding its freshness and glosses,
as if new-dyed not stained with salt.

What can the fairy do but tempt him
with catch-chase and disappearances
until he meets the shining girl?
The silent cinema is full of noises,

cat-calls, whoops and whistles, slurpy
smackers made on hairy backs of arms
when, logwork done and shifting shared,
with the old man's blessing, the couple kiss.

Not much is left. A picnic comes and goes.
A philosopher king forgives his enemies.
A decorated prow appears between the rocks.
All board the ship except the hairy, wide-eyed boy.

MEETING ii

The other time,   the year before   we'd gone to meet
him from the plane   unannounced   and waited
in line with anxious partners   parents   minicab drivers
with felt-tipped guesses at surnames   and when he
wasn't in the queue of faces coming through
we started to look harder   ready to jump   at a shining
forehead   or the glint of thick-lensed spectacles

or at a self-possessed gait   that turned out not to be his

Madly I went to Paddington   thinking he'd passed us
while we were lost in some numb thought
          and of course you found your father
in his flat   he'd by-passed customs like a celebrity
a wheelchair straight to a cab   I'd got the habit
by then of seeming to catch a sight of him
            wasn't that his fawn raincoat in the crowd four or
five heads away   bobbing along at its own pace?

So when we knew we had lost him   after we'd sat
by his hospital bed   looking out   through the night
at the lights coming   on and off   in the tower block
facing   staring at it so long I believed I understood
the lives being lived there   after all that

          I somehow still managed to glimpse him
as I looked up from a book   on a bus ride through Ealing
like a painful afterthought   a sense of something missed

THE BOYS

– reading *Barnaby Rudge*

She recognises this. The widow toiling
wearily along, while the boy *yielding*
to inconstant impulse is *darting,*
flying, lingering. These were his delights
and *she would not have abated them*
by one sad word or murmur.

These boys. Joe sits on his hands, *mumchance,*
– no future but being ordered about;
ravenous Hugh, *set loose* when his mother
broke the law, nurtures dark appetites
in his hidden corner, while Tappertit
snarls *I will be famous yet.*

She thinks of carrot-topped Callum's cackle
of a laugh, cruising into class with his
Porn Star badge, who died in Helmand,
Or doe-eyed Rob – no longer free to stare
out afternoons – who drove into a truck
one month after his sister died.

Or this boy, his low slung pants defying
gravity, his uniform of cool failing
to disguise the anxious eye-darts he flings
about him, telling his young friend. *Don't brag.*
He speaks more softly. *Karma is a bitch.*
She's going to bite your ass.

JUTLAND

'Unhappy and at home' (Seamus Heaney)

i

How often had we wrapped
our mouths around that phrase
in classrooms: *Some day
I will go to Aarhus.*

And here, by Ryanair,
we were, snow still unthawed
at the side of the road,
crocuses and snowdrops

making a stand for life
against the flat green earth
and the solid wall of sky.
The exchange house opened

its doors to us, each in
the white centre of a wall
like openings on a stage
where we'd play another life.

Unlikely tourists among
the warm and brightly clad,
we were looking out for
the stained and peat-brown face

we'd talked about in class.
Out of town at Moesgård
we saw the Grauballe find –
throat slit, smooth, exceptionally

preserved. The museum
could have been the manor-
house hotel from *Festen,*
hiding who knows what hurts.

ii

Afterwards we walked down
to the little stony bay
for our first close look
at the still, cool Baltic.

As for the Tollund Man,
he wasn't to be found in
Aarhus; instead he was
kept near to his digging,

out there in Silkeborg.
We set out on the small
Arriva train, the day
it happened to be shut.

But they let us in, while
they prepared a children's
display of Yggdrasil
and we stood face-to-face

with the foetal body
and its broad sleeping
face that was the spirit
itself of gentleness.

We walked quietly back
past the bobbing pleasure
boats tied up alongside
the out-of-season lake.

iii

The girl on the platform
is setting out from here
with rucksack, wheelie-case
and black portfolio.

The rhythms of their speech
and the familiar sounds
that shape their words persuade
us that we understand

what passes between her
and the others – maybe
neighbours or her mother's
friends. *London*, they say, with

a beam of happiness
for her. This must be where
she is heading, moving
out of the Midlands

town with its small comforts
to a widening world.
They smile as if telling her
she need not be afraid.

CERNUNNOS

Some came in trucks, bedded down as ballast
between the manifold and the manifest,
or in white vans hidden behind white goods,
or clinging on carriage tops to Ebbsfleet.
Others came by sea. Imagine hazel
tarred and twined or wicker threaded into
basket-boats, the recruiting sergeant's shilling,
or furs brought downriver by raft. Then this.

Part of my mind has forgotten itself
already, slipped into the off-white wall
of the interrogation room, finding
faces etched in the floorstains, ready to
be investigated like a fragment
of text scraped onto pottery or bone.

ACCORDING TO JOHN

i

He was playing with one of the birds outside the house,
a partridge maybe, or guinea fowl, *chuck-chuck-chukar*
-chukar it sang; and he crouched throwing seeds to it.
And one of the militia passing on patrol jeered,
Is that how you scholars pass the time? And he said,
looking up at them in the jeep – Didn't the Greeks
say the bird was like a soul? – and – What do any of us
do that's different from digging around in the dust?

Questions. It was always questions with John.

ii

Then there was the story about the bugs. We were
supposed to sleep on pallets in a rough outhouse,
part of a consciousness-raising tour or something.
Yusuf was complaining about bites in the night.
All of us were cold and in need of a wash. And
John put on a grand voice saying – Bugs. Keep
away from us. This mission is sacred. We laughed
and finally got some rest. In the morning he pointed
to the door where the bugs were bunched together.
Was that where the last of the honey was spilled?
He pointed – How creatures obey the voice of a man
when men disobey the commands of their god.

Passive-aggressive, or what?

iii

So the ship, he said, is only safely home
when it comes into the harbour's water
ahead of the storm. And the crop can be
counted on when its harvest is stored in the barn.
The athletes can be proud on the rostrum,
when their medals are fairly won.

Until then, count the risks.

Sadness, the love you have for your children,
your parents' needs, ambition, lack of money,
praise from friends, your youth and health,
beauty, vanity, desire, too much wealth,
short temper, settled hate, promotion,
inertia, idleness, envy of others, possessiveness,
timidity, self-righteous cheek, dishonesty,
did I mention money? the wrong kind of love,
pretentiousness, bad faith...

The obstacles are legion.

Better to enjoy the trip, I thought.

iv

And he could hate well enough.
When the news came of what they'd done
to the body of the girl they killed,
he started giving names to them –
piss-stench, sewer-spewer,
rotten flesh, foul flame-fruit,
tree of burning coals,
dark from within the madness of matter,
neighbour of cancer,
stranger to the holy bath.

We were with him on that.

v

When he talked of his Master, it was never the same.
That was the point, he said.
Sometimes his skin looked soft as a girl's,
though the chest was firm and smooth
when I rested my head there.

James said the Master was like a child,
or a youth with a new beard.
No, said John, the beard was thick and flowing
and on top his hair was already receding.
How the light shone back at us from the wise wide forehead.

vi

When they took him in, John said,
I was scared and ran away.
Holed up in a cave in the hills for a while.
Then in the half-light a figure came.
That wasn't me they got, said the Master.
That was the other man you sometimes glimpsed.
That was a cross of wood, but this is a cross of light.

John pointed to the sky and talked
like some scientist from CERN
about energy and matter and light,
wholeness and singularity,
the root of things, the left hand and the right.

vii

And that's how it was in those days,
we'd sit on the steps of that old ruin
near Selçuk and listen to traveller's tales.
There was the one we called Sun-Ra,
the no-meat man, back from his overland trip
to Kabul, Lahore and all points East.
There are many gods he'd say
but only one source of light.
Care for each other, like these sparrows do.

So it was, in those days
by the old temple of Artemis.
And some of us dressed like those men.
Some of us followed their diets.

Some of us learned their rites
or wrote out their sayings.
Some followed their words hoping to better their lives.
Some used their power to enslave.

viii

He was playing with one of the birds outside the house,
a partridge maybe, or guinea fowl, *chuck-chuck-chukar*
-chukar it sang; and he crouched throwing seeds to it,
stroked and ruffled its feathers. One of the patrol passing
asked, Is that how you wise men pass the time?
He looked over at them, That rifle over your shoulder,
do you always keep it cocked and ready to shoot?

I don't remember what he answered,
but the fighting goes on.

HIS GRANDSON CONSIDERS THE PHILOSOPHY OF MARTIN HEIDEGGER

Being here
is full of wonder, yes –
the tastes of banana or broccoli
the noise I make with my finger on my lips
and faces to look at, not mine.

Does the Sandman puppet
feel what I feel
when a you goes away?
I don't think so.

If I put a triangle block
in the triangle window,
or a round block in the round hatch
of the shape-sorting house,
that is correct.

But the doubled image of me
in the strengthened window glass
is not correct, but true.
I laugh at the truth.
I clap my hands.

TAKING DOWN THE STATUE

Crossing Cavendish Square
in my lunch break, my new
umbrella just holding out
against the wind, I sniff
something strange from the
dripping, cream-coloured
equestrian statue I hardly
noticed until now.
                    Turning back
to read the caption on
the plinth, I see that this
is an installation made
four years ago, designed
to last twelve months –
Written in Soap by the
sculptor Meekyoung Shin.
It's made of soap.

                    And, while
the horse's flank still holds
its muscled curves
and even the rider's head
is more or less intact,
the forelegs have slid
away, revealing the
supportive metal struts
of the armature.
                    The 'butcher
of Culloden', Cumberland
took personal responsibility,
after the battle, for checking
the fallen, sorting the rebels
from the uniformed soldiers

and seeing that each was
clubbed, or stabbed or shot.

After that the Clearances.

                         And later,
in 'honor to his publick virtue',
and 'private kindnesses'
the statue in lead and gilt
of this younger son to the king.
Poised on his prancing
horse, the conquering hero
looked out at the shifting
London scene for almost
a century. Taken down,
in 1866, as an offence
to public taste.
              The soap horse
starts to look like a victim
of atrocity.
              I suppose
the Korean sculptor
who made this replica
knew something of
division, occupation
and distrust. In this square
behind John Lewis,
she lets us see
how passing time
erodes the waxy pomp
of power, leaving –
in what's left of
last night's storm –
a faint perfume
of cleansing.

HENRY HARCLAY'S *ORDINARY QUESTIONS*

It was known
that Alexander
had fixed gates
across the chasm
east of the Caspian sea
that enclosed
those almost people
who performed
abominations:
foetus-eaters,
dog-men
and the rest.

And it was known
if even one
got through
those gates
(made by the
welding of two
mountains)
it would be
a signal
of end times
of final reckoning
and judgement.

Harclay
who had studied
with Scotus in
Paris noted
that Tartars
Magyars and
Mongols had
worked their way
through that
passage for
seven centuries
at least.

The end times
were a long
time coming.

RECENT EVENTS IN LOGRES

'And Merlin slept, who had imagined her
Of water-sounds and the deep unsoundable swell
A creature to bewitch a sorcerer,
And lay there now within her towering spell.'

– Richard Wilbur

i

As a boy he would sit under the rowan tree
listening to his mother's prayers. Let him not
favour his father. Keep him from darkness.

Small and silent he kept to the edges,
noting patterns in the leaves and branches,
as daylight left, tracing roads between the stars.

ii

The father was a shadow in the darkness,
a memory of a memory, a tale of power.

So power lay in him as in his father,
a mark of pride, a thing to fear.

iii

At two he broke his silence to tell them
the exact number of leaves in his tree.

At five he drew down curses by guessing
the day of the week on which his mother was born.

At eight he was sent to the priest.

iv

And Blaise was full of wonder at the stories
the boy told him – that were beautiful
and seemed good and true. He took pains
to write them down in the boy's own words.

There was the tale of the fatherless boy
brought to the king when the tower collapsed.
Rather than spill my blood. he said,
listen to my tale of what's under the tower.

He told them two dragons danced in war
there – on a lake that shone with fire.
Vortigen withdrew his troops,
leaving the boy to claim the land.

v

And in the stories he became that boy.
He saw that magic crewless ship
caught in a cleft on a wilderness isle,
the red wood and the green wood and the white,
all splinters from the tree of life.

He saw in each man's eyes his fate,
who'd win in battle or in love.
He became the power inside the power,
servant to the leader he mastered.
They said the wise man had his master's ear.

What could Arthur do but listen to the man
who said who'd take the perilous seat
and who would suffer the dolorous stroke;
who'd known when and how he would be born
and, he guessed, had in mind how he'd end.

vi

Those were high days for horse-backed men,
leather and metal clad, cunningly armed,
venturing out to boast their strength
and dazzle the eyes of boys and women.

How did they get their power?
The priest said at first all were equal:
children of a single father and mother.
But envy and desire took might for right.

These became our champions,
defending the weak against the strong.
Myrdinn gave Blaise a straight look.
How could he tell the two apart?

vii

How could he tell them apart?
The envious fiends.
The beloved protectors.

Rushing around the countryside,
in gouge-fests and ravishings,
their cap-badge slogans blazoned:

THE LAND ABOVE ALL;
FOR GOD'S SAKE ONLY;
DEATH BEFORE QUESTIONS;
HOMELAND SECURITY.

viii

Lancelot revealed that the Lady had told him
(despite her weak understanding) that the noble
and gentle were ranked above the rest
for their strength, their boldness, their good looks,
their exquisite manners and philanthropic deeds.
This is why we bow to them, she had said.
They were men who would not hesitate to judge
or act their judgements out, decisively with blows.

ix

Beside that noisy glamour, in Carleon or Winchester,
an unpresuming man could sneak away,
find quiet by the seashore or by the river's edge.

He was there and not there.
He spoke little but he spoke with weight.
He was reported in different towns on the same day.

Easy then to be known as somehow uncanny,
to go unrecognised and taken for a shape-shifter.
Now like a child. Now like a man of fourscore.

x

He spoke little but he spoke with weight.

Young Arthur took out his sword
and held its brilliance in the evening light
with a lover's excitement,
dreaming glory and his name.

And Myrdinn's counsel:
Look to your scabbard; it's worth ten swords.
Keep your scabbard with you.
Prefer the scabbard and save your blood.

He hadn't thought someone like Viviane could appear.
There she was in the wood: washing and laughing
      by the spring.

He stared at her a long time before he said a word.
He feared he might lose his wisdom or do something
      to shame her.

She was a vavasour's daughter, raised in a manor.
He was a wandering apprentice in the art of illusion.

Show me, she asked. He made a circle in the ground
and with his eyes and his words, invited into the space

tumblers, lute-players, acrobatic dancers, musclemen,
a magic-lanternist, someone to draw her portrait,

flower arrangers, fashionistas, designers of fantasy
castles, aerialists and finally an orchard replete

with apples, nectarines, hazelnuts, filberts, figs.
If you favour me, he said, I will tell you

how all this is done. You can write it down
so that any who like may understand, and

know I have the will and heart to do you well.
As he spoke, the circus figures and paper castles

began to fade, though the fruit remained.
How did you know I could read and write,

she puzzled, only now suspicious.
I can teach you my art, he said.

xii

This was in the forest at the start of autumn,
under the shade of a darkening beech.

He would show her where a spring might start
or how to turn a stream a different way.

And all the while they loved and lay together.
He promised to return before midsummer day.

xiii

He offered prophecies to pass the time.

Virgo lets droop its maiden blossoms
and the Pleiades burst into tears.
None returns to the duty expected of it.

A tree will spring up on top of the Tower of London.
Native birds will lose their power of flight,
and acorns burgeon on the lime trees' boughs.

Fish will die because of the heat in the River Usk.
The Forest of Dean will awake and burst into human speech.

Monks in their cowls will be forced into marriage,
and their cries heard on the peaks of the Alps.

I could go on all day like this, he says.

xiv

He dropped these into the talk that drifted around the
        great table, swaggering, romancing, mystical talk:
of raids, fixed battles and strategic retreats in wars with
        the Romans and Saxons;
of challenges met on the road;
of masked or visored strangers whose names must be
        guessed from their shields' iconography, or the slit
        of eyes between the hood and the nose-piece;
of beguiling women whose desires and motives were a
        shimmering unknown – islands glimpsed looking
        into a setting sun;
of loyalty and brotherhood, jealousy and betrayal;
of visions and a quest, of hidden truths and the relic of
        a sacred past.

xv

In the peace after some great battle
they would sit down with fighters from Gaul or Armorica,
servants of the King of Orkney, Irishmen or Danes,
and share their stories.

So Merdynn remembered the Breton Tale
of the two lovers in the vale of Pîtres.
To marry the king's daughter
the young man must carry her to the mountain top.
Her lover was small of frame,
so she fasted and wore only her thinnest shift.
His heart raced as he carried her
only to burst on the final ridge.

And the story too of Odd and Oldmar,
the Viking and the Irish girl
who made the raider a shirt,
though he was her father's killer,
to save her village. She sang how
it was spun from six lands' silk
and he that it slipped snugly to him
stronger than the frost of chain-mail.

He thought again of Viviane
the pain and delight of love.

xvi

There were stories of love nearby.
Lancelot's passion followed its own rules:
certain, determined, unconsidered.

Wounded and in disguise,
he still caught the eyes
of the fair maid of Ascalot.

Blushing as a flower,
weeping on the hour,
her only cure was Lancelot.

So the song went. And the queen
saw the funeral barge drift downriver,
her own lover's shield next to the foolish girl.
And hadn't Gawain told her
the maid's own words?
For his leman he hath me take.

Lancelot must be exiled from her love.

xvii

Merdynn began to sense an end to things.
Agravain muttering about honour.
A pyre built ready for the queen.
Lancelot in Benoic on the Loire.

Gawain and Arthur abroad
to find revenge and Mordred
ready to fill the gap…

xviii

Now it was time to slip once
more between the trees, to say
farewell to Blaise and slide
into the forest of Brocéliande.

The rain on the broad leaves
whispered like the rumour
of a stream and small birds
chattered at his passing.

Tints of copper and gold
as the autumn evening
spread before him like a
long, unearned reward.

xix

Viviane was learned as any clerk or cloistered copyist.
Waiting by the appointed oak, she thought over the past:
what he'd taught her and what she still would need to know.

She put her arms around his neck and loved the face she saw,
lined as a forest leaf. 'I want to know', she said, 'the spell to keep you here,
imprisoned in beauty, in a tower without walls'.

And he, 'I could build that tower, here'. And she,
'No, teach me how to do it and I'll make a home here
to our liking, where you may do my will as I do yours'.

She listened to his words and wrote them down.
They wandered hand in hand throughout the wood,
resting by a high hawthorn bush loaded with blossom.

He lay his head in her lap and slept. Carefully she rose,
took off her headscarf and used the pleated end
to draw a circle in the earth around that tree. She sang

and when he woke, they lay in a stately bed
inside a towering palace he could not leave.
She came and went, but mostly chose to stay.

xx

Gawainet was sent to search him out.

He found only a wall of mist
and a voice caught inside the air,
counting the leaves, praising his love,
preparing to become unknown.

MIDNIGHT OIL

No moon. Light from the
anglepoise. Bashō open
face down on the desk.

THE TRIUMPH OF ORTHODOXY

For perhaps too long, she said,
we have been following The Word,
only offered the distraction
of decorating it with goldfoil
or voicing elaborate geometries
with its vowels. Is this the time
to proceed down the aisle with
many-coloured banners,
bereft of fable or command?

Their colours are split sunset
or Mary's blue and they are
shaped to the human face,
faces that look forward, whose
high cheekbones, olive-dark
eyes flesh forth a presence
that touches us, that we would
touch in turn, a doorway
to an unimagined beyond.

So let us close the book
and turn instead to miracles
of handiwork, to paint and dye
matched to the warp of a board
prepared with red clay, honey
egg and wine. Only then
might words rise in the mind
– as vermilion, cadmium,
cobalt and ultramarine.

MEETING iii

in your author photograph   white-haired
white-bearded   dapper in a white jacket
your head back as you look   sagely towards us
     leaning on a crash barrier near St Pancras
you're on the move again   Paris to
Sheffield this time   another year Dublin
or Mozambique

                talking and walking

like our first conversation
             all the way from your
West London reading to your Manchester train

then I hadn't uncovered   your double identity
prised apart the scholar from the   legendary
sheet-metal worker
         the persona from
the disguise   picked up in transit
from Montserrat to Notting Hill   Tirana
to Hull   Cologne to Coleraine
Provence (house-building)   to Port Moresby
('where I was the government')

few meetings   but enough to make a friendship
a party in Greenwich   a festival at Hallam

and that long afternoon in Paris   above the canal
your memories and indiscretions   rolling out
in laughing outrage at the absurd   the pompous
the unkind   the smarts you rose above
but did not hide

          I was waiting for your article about
the retired professor's life   the anglophone
bookshops   when we heard
your heart gave way   you died alone
In Tooting we stood at the back   of the
Methodist Church   hearing the sirens rage
when they brought your small casket
                              of ashes   home

TWILIGHT AT FOUR

Molly watches as the tall striped sky
turns grey above the river and the railway tracks.

She knows this is the town she'll move from,
following the telegraph wires and the lines
of migrating birds. The copper trees envy
her her hair. She'll leave the trees behind.

Where Harry stands, you can see behind
the new-built flats not, as you first thought,
a sky stiff as an ironed sheet but a white
smudged with shifting stains where you track
patches of dark and light like clothes on a line.

What she likes is: they don't ask where she's from.
It's not her wish to probe behind
a space as lightly peopled as the sky
revealed in those enticing gaps between
the naked twigs of wind-stripped trees.

Harry constructs a history of trees.

From empty spaces along the forest tracks
or from how the higher branches slide behind
each other trailing down the sullen sky, he
tells the fortune of the forest – as if lines
on an opened palm.
                              She rehearses lines
she hoped to improvise, sitting under trees,
on a park bench against the city sky.

Both know something someday will emerge from
what has always been here beneath the sky,
patterned like leaves of the large trees behind.

NOT YET

Quite often now
some thought or
observation rises
yet fails to find
itself in speech.

Reticence. Or
else the *mot juste*
just deserts me.
I'm memorially
lacunose.

These two,
conversely,
enter the symbolic
order with a certain
bounce and verve.

One spells out the
names on coat pegs
or announces prices
on the minimarket
shelves.

His brother points
at me: *gada? gaga?*
Not yet a name
I answer to, but
getting close.

POLITICS

There are small red hearts on your blouse
and your heart is on your sleeve
as you address the council chamber.

Sitting here on the balcony
my attention is fixed.

VIEWLESS WINGS

The lift to this level
opens at a reception
desk where a monitor
notes investment
opportunities arising
from the Australian
floods. The door to
the cloakroom is tall
enough to enter on a
horse. We are meeting
in an office high
above the trading floor,
but you can glimpse
it far down in the atrium.

In what was a war-time
fighter-base and is
now an open prison,
a trainee barista
prepares our paninis.
While we congratulate
the award winner,
men in lime-green
slacks circle in small
groups catching then
avoiding eyes, as
scampering rabbits
jump and burrow
inside the fence.

'But writing has
taken us places',
I say to him as we
leave the ceremony,
even if we're only
two that will do
to swell a crowd
or eat a canapé,
but he is already
pacing the riverpath
near Wapping, lines
arranging themselves
patiently beneath
waves of white hair.

12 X 12

i

A squirrel
has been scrumping
small apples from
the stunted tree.

It hasn't
ever made a
crop that we could
take pleasure in.

He looks from side
to side, rapidly;
taking what he can,
then moving on.

ii

Mark Rothko
used turpentine
to thin the strong
colours he chose.

So the paint
would stain, more than
coat, the tightly
stretched canvasses.

Each of them
larger than a man
with arms outstretched.
Filling the walls.

iii

In a Walm
Lane shop window
bright African
textiles dazzle.

A startling
geometry
turns a teardrop
to smiling lips.

A blackboard
with figures on,
for a lucky girl
going to school.

iv

The boy on
the platform is
enjoying his
loud game. His hand

opens to
cover the fist's
stone. Stone smashes
fingers' scissors.

No-one is
keeping the score,
but his shouts insist
he is winning.

v

To get this
news by email
is bad enough
but the person

I wished that
I could talk to
about your death
has also gone.

I picture you
– that gesture.
Spreading your hands
as you start to sigh.

vi

Seeing the
ladder from this
side, we catch a
gleam on the bald

downcast head
of the workman
holding the huge
iron pliers.

A painting of
an ordinary man
doing the job
no-one else wants.

vii

Returning
through the streets
I remember
from an evening

long ago,
it's easy to
recall faces
and tones of voice

— but the shop
that should be at
the walk's end is
suddenly not there.

viii

What was it
brought back to life
this sharp sense of
boyhood's hot tears

— not grazed knees
or cruel words
but injustice,
the unearned slap

unthought-of
for years, but real
now — walking through
the underpass?

ix

Consider
me to be an
ambassador
for history.

I record
sense and nonsense,
what continues,
the latest trend.

Some of it
I will never grasp.
But I gather the
evidence.

x

The herbal teas
I sometimes use
to make drinks on
sleepless nights

list arcane
ingredients:
tulsi leaf, lime-
flower, valerian;

I store them
in a tin marked
Absinthe – an adept
of decadence.

xi

Abū Manşūr
gives us fourteen
different names
for the clouds.

These include
a cloud which may
inundate or
bring no rain at all.

I lap this up
cat-like. Imagine
a black cloud, its
nose streaked with cream.

xii

In the park
a small white dog
is barking at the
foot of a tree.

Sitting here,
I'm tempted to
appropriate
his energy.

The bright fleeting
thing outruns my thought.
I may have chosen
the wrong tree.

LOOSE LEAF

These old green or orange
paperbacks are falling
apart on us. Pages
dropping out, tobacco-
coloured, flaking at the
edges. Incipient
autumn is outside us
too: the bright yellow slips
of willow, or still green
oak-leaves curling as if
left too near the fire. The
low afternoon sun warm on
the back of the neck throws
light on the spire across
the road and the white rose
among the tight black curls
of the schoolgirl checking
her smartphone. In the park
there is time to admire
flashes of yellow and
red on the beak of this
coot-like bird and marvel
at the gloriousness
of now, unbothered
by the evening's chill.

A TRUE STORY

Up! High! The child laughs pointing through the window
      at the two birds in the guttering that runs under
      the grey slate roof.

The white bird with its mobile head monitoring the street;
      the young grey-feathered bird scuttering end-to-end.

'The situation is beyond control', Councillor Brown (Locals
      First) addresses the meeting. He need not remind them
      of the incident at the harbour.

'We want our town back', he is sputtering, scanning the hall.
      'The time has come for a cull!'

The white herring gull is dragging a knotted white plastic bag
      from the fly-tipped pile behind the disused phone-box
      pulling and scratching as it goes.

It takes four gulls screeching and tugging to tear it apart
      and feast on the leftover Chinese takeaway.

Miss Dawson (Liberal Elect) reminded the meeting of the
      recent oil spillage. The effort and expense
      undertaken in the aftermath.

Cleaning feathers with a toothbrush and detergent.
      'Surely this showed us at our best?'

GPS tracking of birds in the town revealed a nesting
      site in the cinema currently showing
      Finding Dory.

The gull population, which is native not migratory,
consists of 239 breeding pairs.

Doctor Triomphe (Third Way) offered the assembly
his preferred solution: a transparent ceiling.
A dome of rare device:

using recycling technology, guano a key constituent.
The gulls would pay for the roof!

Ha-ha-ha!   *Meeeeww!*   *Ha-ha-ha! Ha-ha-ha!*
    Keow!   *Keow!*
    Huoh-huoh-huoh.

Klee-ew?   *Klee-ew?*   *Ha-ha-ha! Ha-ha-ha!*
    Meeeeww!   *Huoh-huoh-huoh.*

OFFSHORE

'Ahoy', the sailor calls, '*Ahoj!*'
paddling his kayak downriver
a million metres from the sea.
Are those gulls or swifts following him
shadowed by the repurposed tower?

In the stone town, arches of stone
fan out above with peach shades
of sunlight streaming through the glass.
It is a long afternoon but not endless.

Look here is a picture of Barbara
Radziwill – pale, bejewelled and
not long to live. And, look, the ash
of Monet's cigarette refuses
to fall as he outstares his canvas.

The girls and boys of the village
rocked in their two-seater swings.
The city's steam-whistle reached them
slowly through the woods and lanes.

Our bridges cross rivers whose courses
have shifted. Warehouses turn into galleries.
It's pleasing to loosen the ties
of where we came from, replacing *syke*
and *sheugh* with *biro, brio, samizdat.*

Memorial plaques glitter in the
gap-toothed streets of renamed districts.
We follow the shifting electric display
spread out in the blood-streaked sky.

Hoardings appear with dates picked out
in a lightbulb array. 1848 and
Lajos Kossuth feels the century
turning against him. 1898 and
General Blanco announces *El Desastre*.

And Jean-Jacques is still botanizing near
Ménilmontant, caught in a reverie
between that which is no longer
and that which is often not to be.

How can one not look back on the
closed train, the manifesto lacking
a clause, an advancing *popolo*
chanting to an old Lombard tune?
Glories lost to a poundshop Gloriana.

Where are the accordions and clarinets
or has something already happened
so we hardly recognise these buildings:
town hall, hospital and school?

Why only trombones and a bass
drum, as we view from the stern
of the ferry the coastline slipping away?

NEW BUILD

Between developments
of industrial sites,

we are stilled by a bush
vivid with green

from which the jargon
of small birds bursts

with a sudden
playground shriek.

Tits and finches
rise in numbers

gathering like buds
on the almost empty

branches of a birch.
And what to do but

laugh at such evidence
of determined life?

A NOTE ON SOURCES

The painted fan on which 'Fan-piece' is based, appeared in the exhibition *Masterpieces of Chinese Painting: 700–1900* (Victoria & Albert Museum, 2013).

'A Floating Life' is structured following the divisions of Shen Fu's memoir, *Six Records of a Floating Life*.

Events in 'At the Coast' take place in the following locations: Studland Point, Crackington Haven, Mumbles, Caswell Bay, Swanage, Kinghorn in Fife, Whitstable, Lulworth Cove, Margate, Eastbourne, then (after an inland excursion to Paris including a passage from Mallarmé's 'Brise Marine') Llanmadoc, Rotherslade, St Ives and the Old Harry Rocks in Purbeck. I first heard the story of the coastal erosion in Hallsands from the television documentary series *Coast*, a favourite of my mother's. Alfred Sisley's paintings of South Wales were exhibited in the National Gallery in 2008.

'Weemoed' draws on the *Letters of Vincent Van Gogh* and Steven Naifeh & Gregory White Smith's *Van Gogh: the Life*.

'Taking Down the Statue' describes *Written in Soap*, an installation made by the sculptor Meekyoung Shin.

I read about Henry Harclay's *Ordinary Questions* in *The Edges of the Medieval World* (edited by Gerhard Juritz and Julian Kreen, published by the University of Central Europe).

The major source for 'Recent Events in Logres' is the legend of Merlin in the Vulgate Cycle. It also draws on Geoffrey of Monmouth's *History of the Kings of Britain*, the Breton Lais of Marie de France, the metrical romance *Le Morte Arthur* and the Örvar-Odds saga.

'According to John' makes use of *The Acts of John* from the New Testament Apocrypha in MR James's translation and accounts of the life of Appolonius of Tyana.

'The Triumph of Orthodoxy' alludes to the restoration of icons to the Eastern Church in 843 after a period of iconoclasm.

'12 x 12' attempts and probably distorts the Korean Sijo form. It contains references to paintings by Mark Rothko from the Royal Academy's *Abstract Expression* exhibition and by Luca Signorelli in the National Gallery. The African fabrics were in the window of Metro Textiles in Willesden. The remark about clouds can be found in Shihab Al-Din Al-Nuwayri's *The Ultimate Ambition in the Arts of Erudition*.

ACKNOWLEDGEMENTS

Some of these poems appeared previously in print or online in the following places: *Ambit, Bare Fiction, Envoi, The High Window, Live Canon 2017, Long Poem Magazine, New Boots and Pantisocracies, New Walk, North, Poetry London, The Poetry School, Shearsman, Verse Daily, Verse Kraken, The Warwick Review* and *York Literary Review*.

Other poems first appeared in the anthologies *A Mutual Friend: Poems for Charles Dickens* (Two Rivers Press, 2011), and *Nosh* (Two Rivers Press, 2017). 'Cernunnos' was commissioned by Bank Street Arts for the exhibition *In Their Own Words* (2008) as a response to an artwork of that name by Iwan Bala.

My thanks to Todd Swift, Edwin Smet and all the Eyewear team for their support in the preparation of this volume.

**EYEWEAR** PUBLISHING